Election 2016
The Year We Gave Up
A Coloring Book For Upset Voters

Todd Kale

&

Dave Metrick

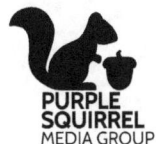

**PURPLE
SQUIRREL**
MEDIA GROUP

Purple Squirrel Media
San Diego, California
www.purplesquirrelmedia.net

ISBN-10: 0-9965033-2-3
ISBN-13: 978-0-9965033-2-7

DEDICATION:

We'd like to dedicate this book to the poorly educated, misinformed American electorate. Your ignorance has made the 2016 presidential race (and this snarky coloring book) a shameful reality.

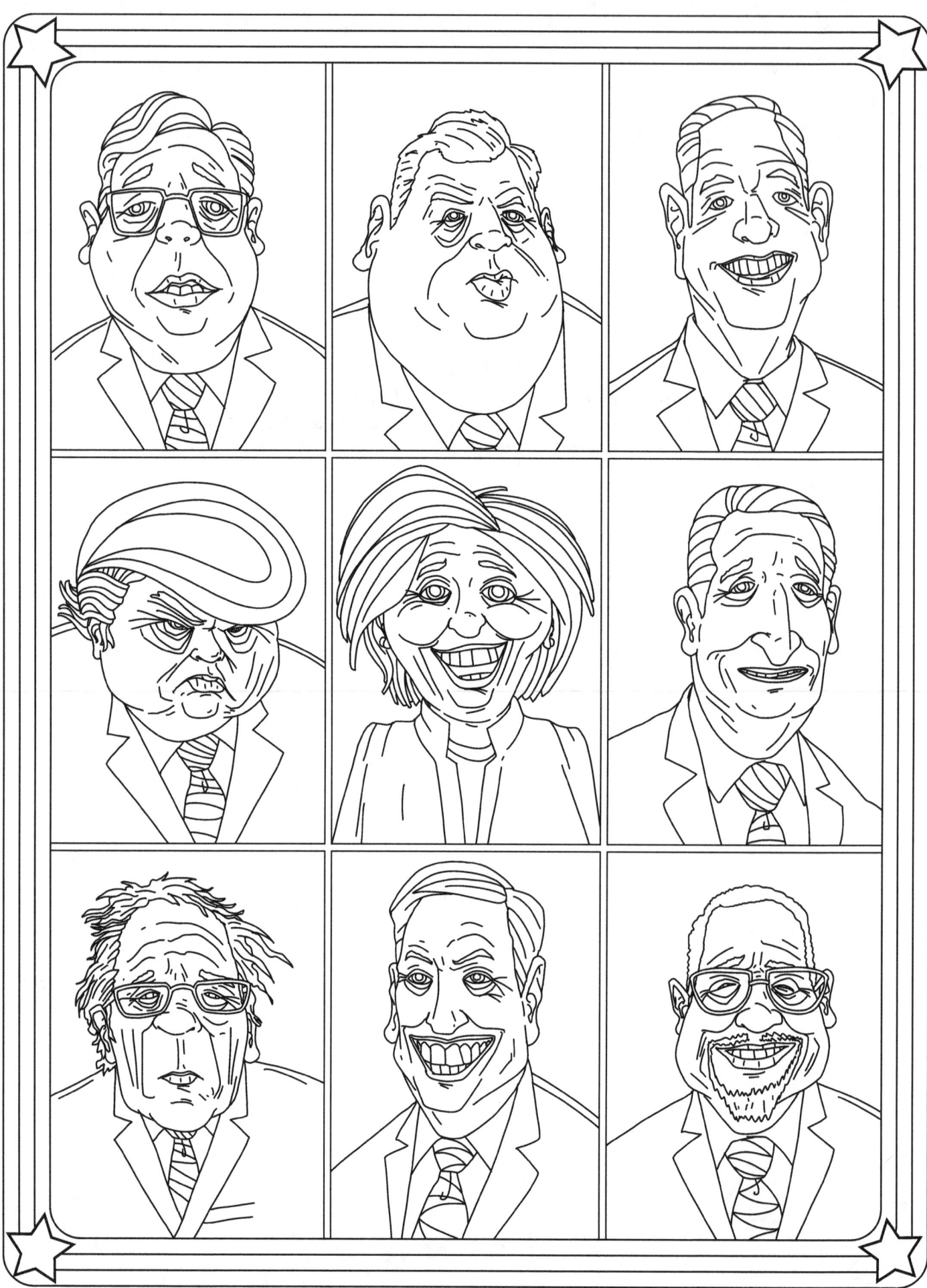

INTRODUCTION:

Every four years a relatively small percentage of the American population gets together and elects someone to boldly lead us into the future. The most recent cycle of presidential hopefuls has produced such cartoony, two-dimensional characters we felt it only natural to render their exaggerated likenesses for your coloring enjoyment.

"I color outside of the lines...
because I'm not some kind of Washington insider."

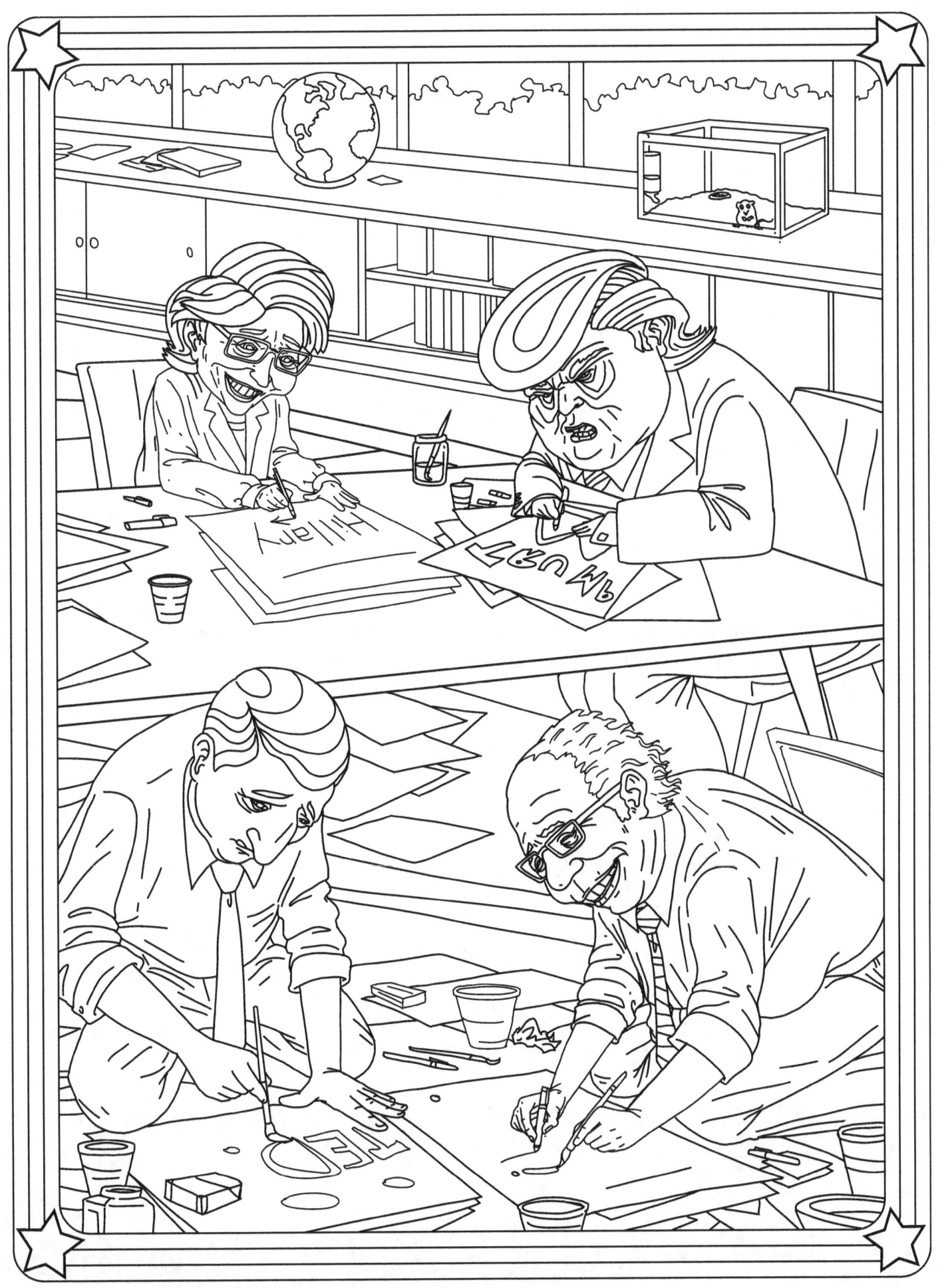

"Stay tuned for the latest in the 2016 presidential primaries...
but mostly news about Donald Trump."

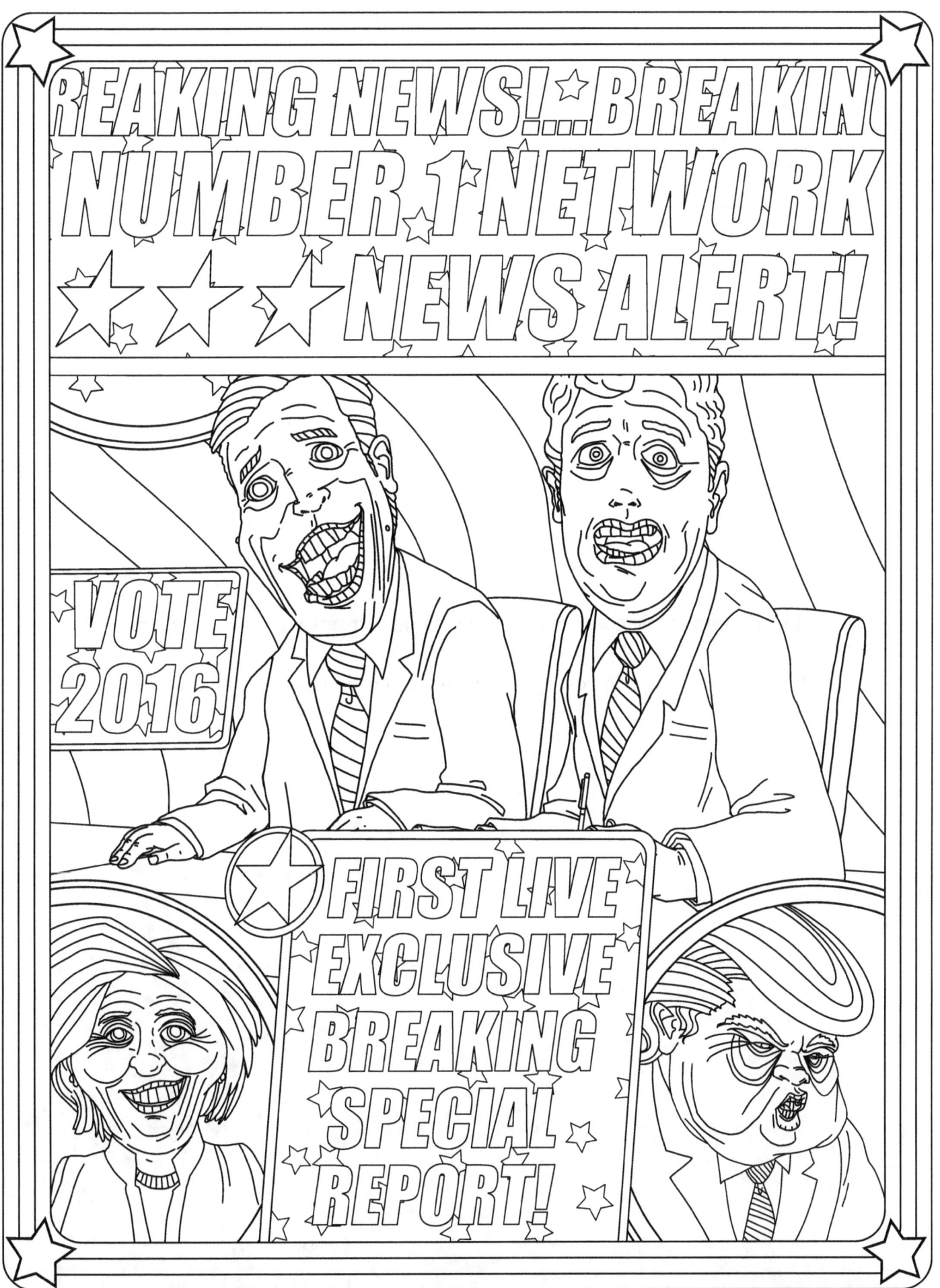

"¡Ha! ¡El hombre de color naranja piensa que vamos a pagar la factura!"

(Translation – Ha! The orange man thinks we're going to pay the bill!)

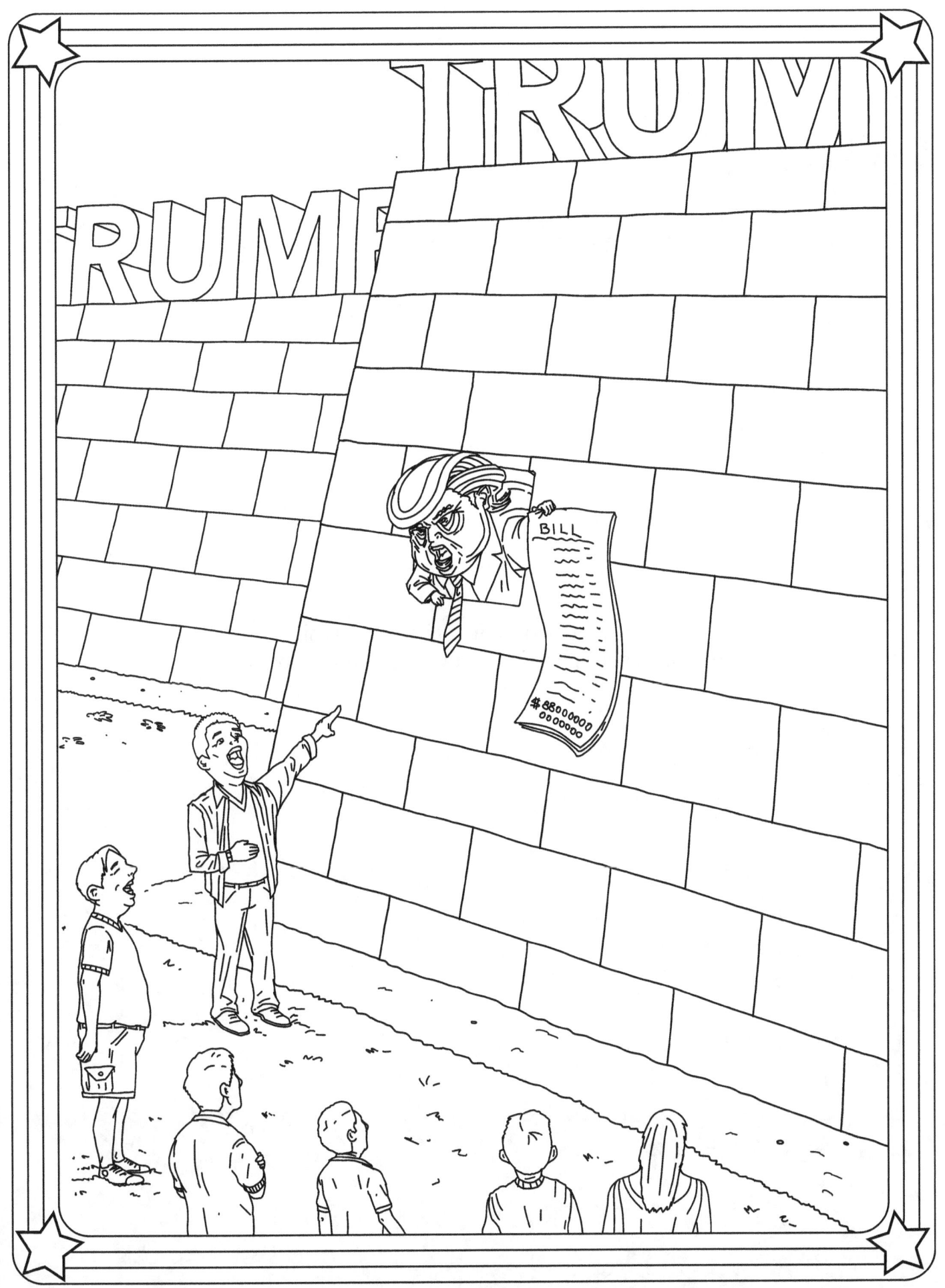

"The White House just got a lot classier.
I'm putting a gold-plated hot tub in the Lincoln bedroom."

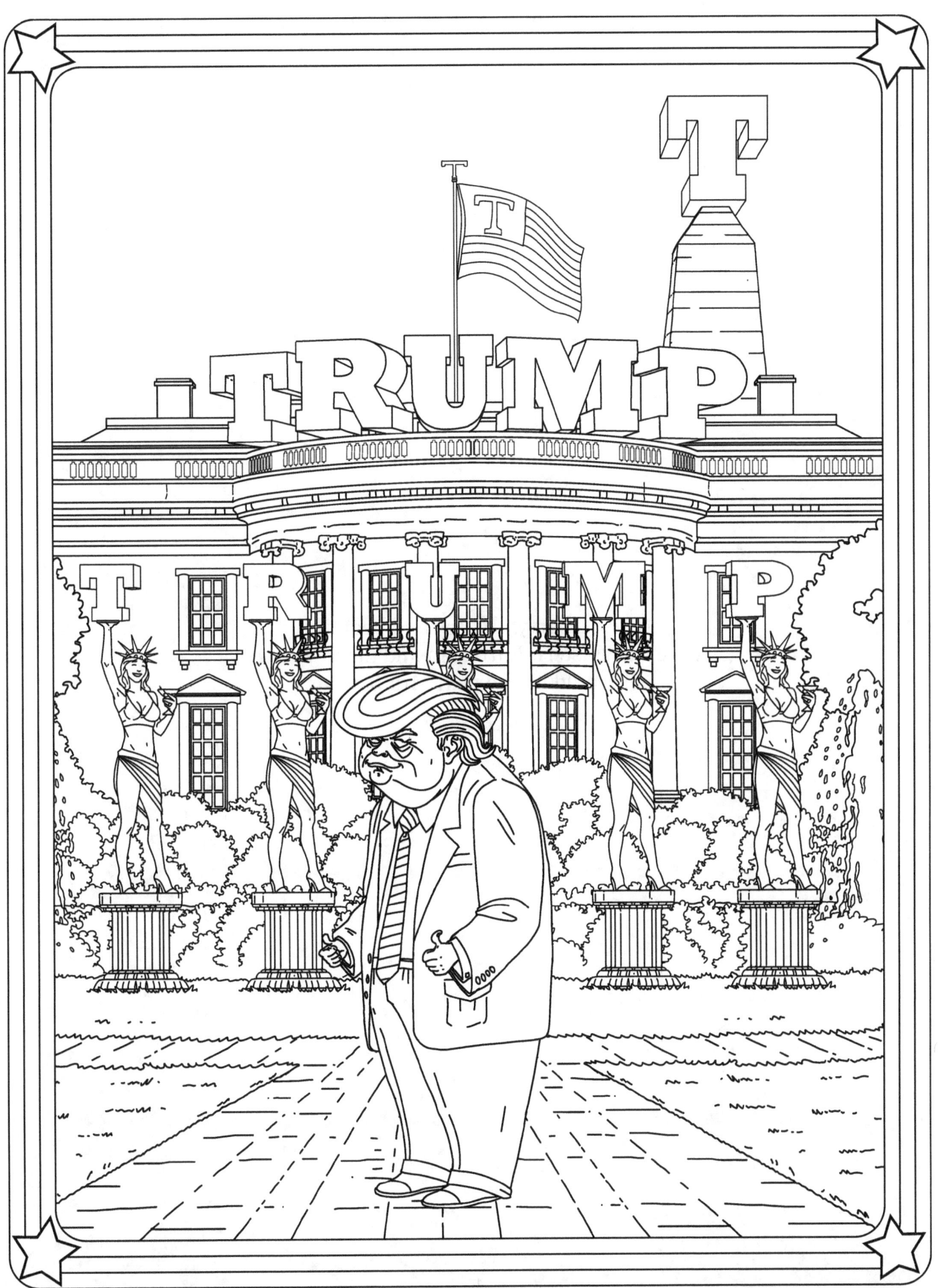

"Lady Liberty... classy and beautiful.
If she was Eastern European and much younger,
she could be the next Mrs. Trump."

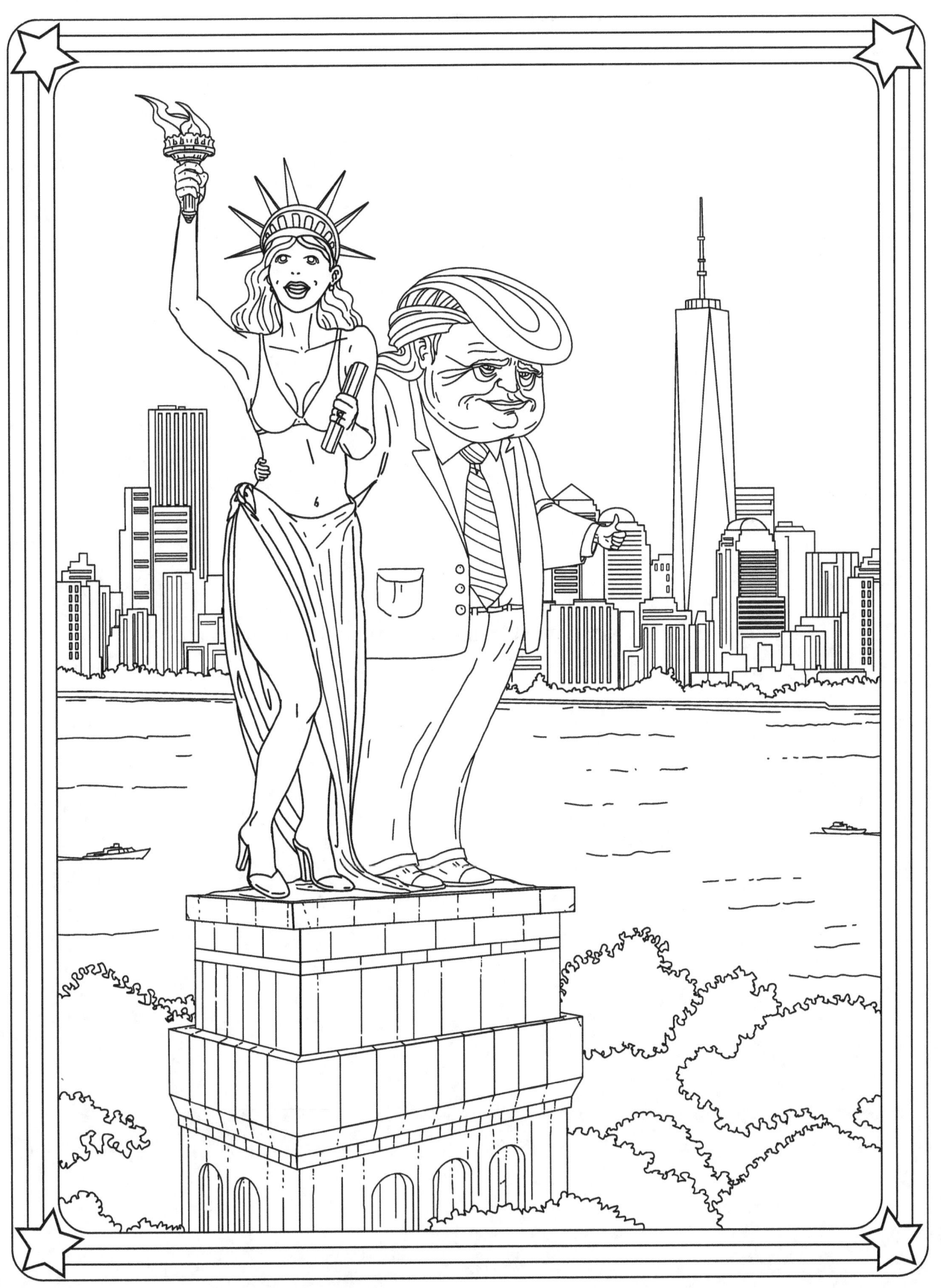

"I have the classiest, most tremendous thoughts in my head.
The best thoughts!"

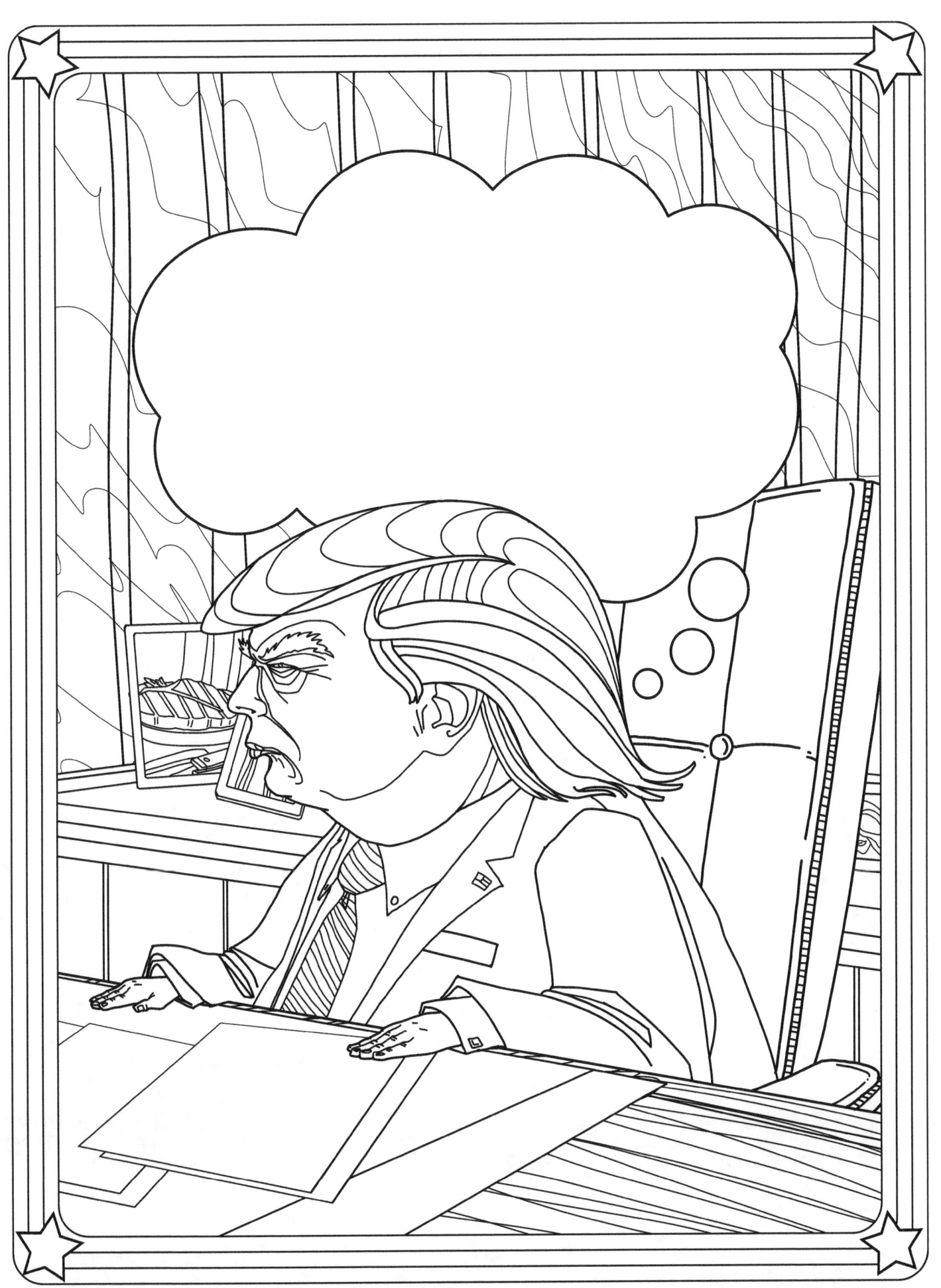

"Trump Bald Eagles are the highest quality, best eagles money can buy."

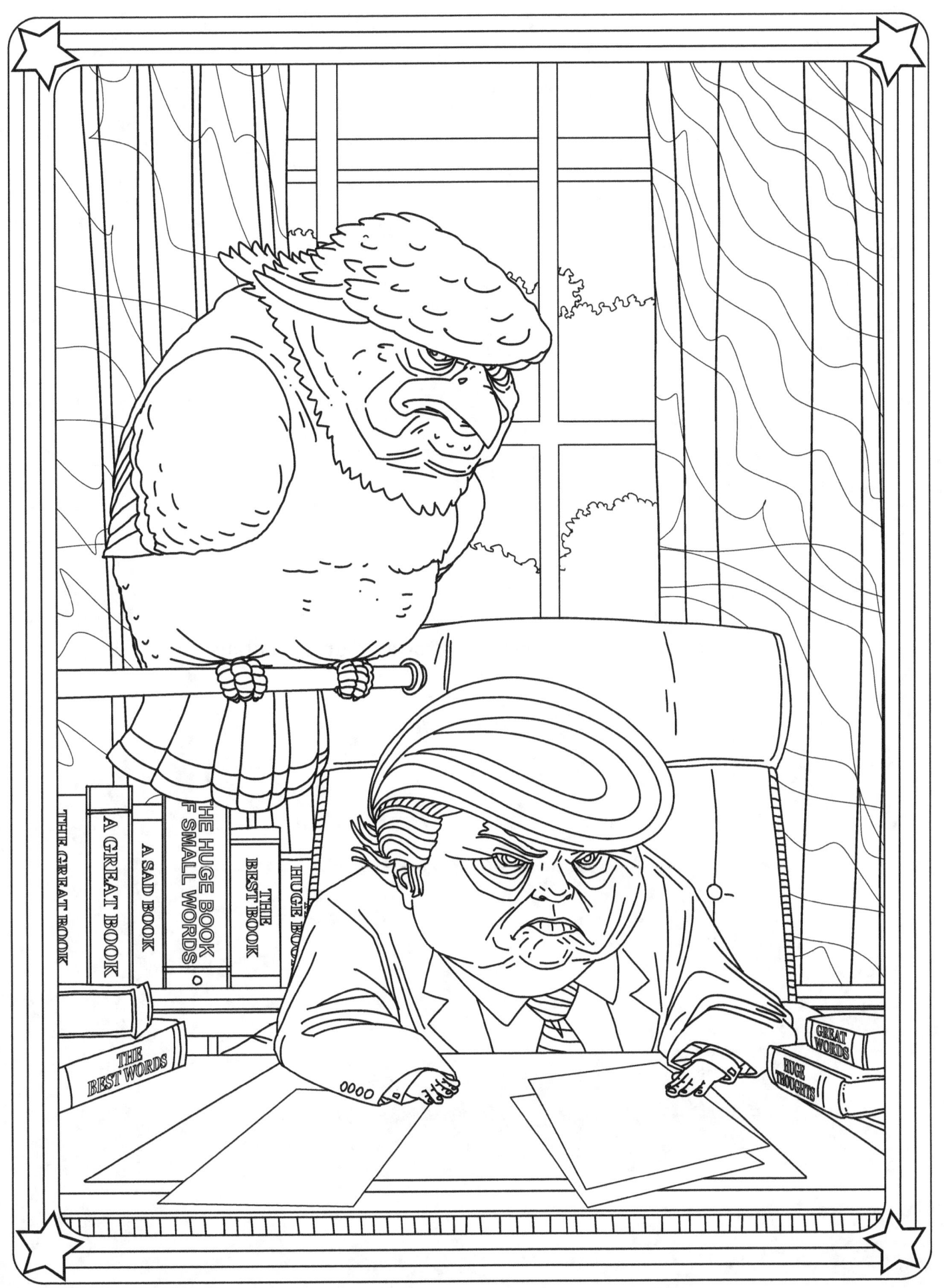

"Write what I want or I'm taking away your credentials!"

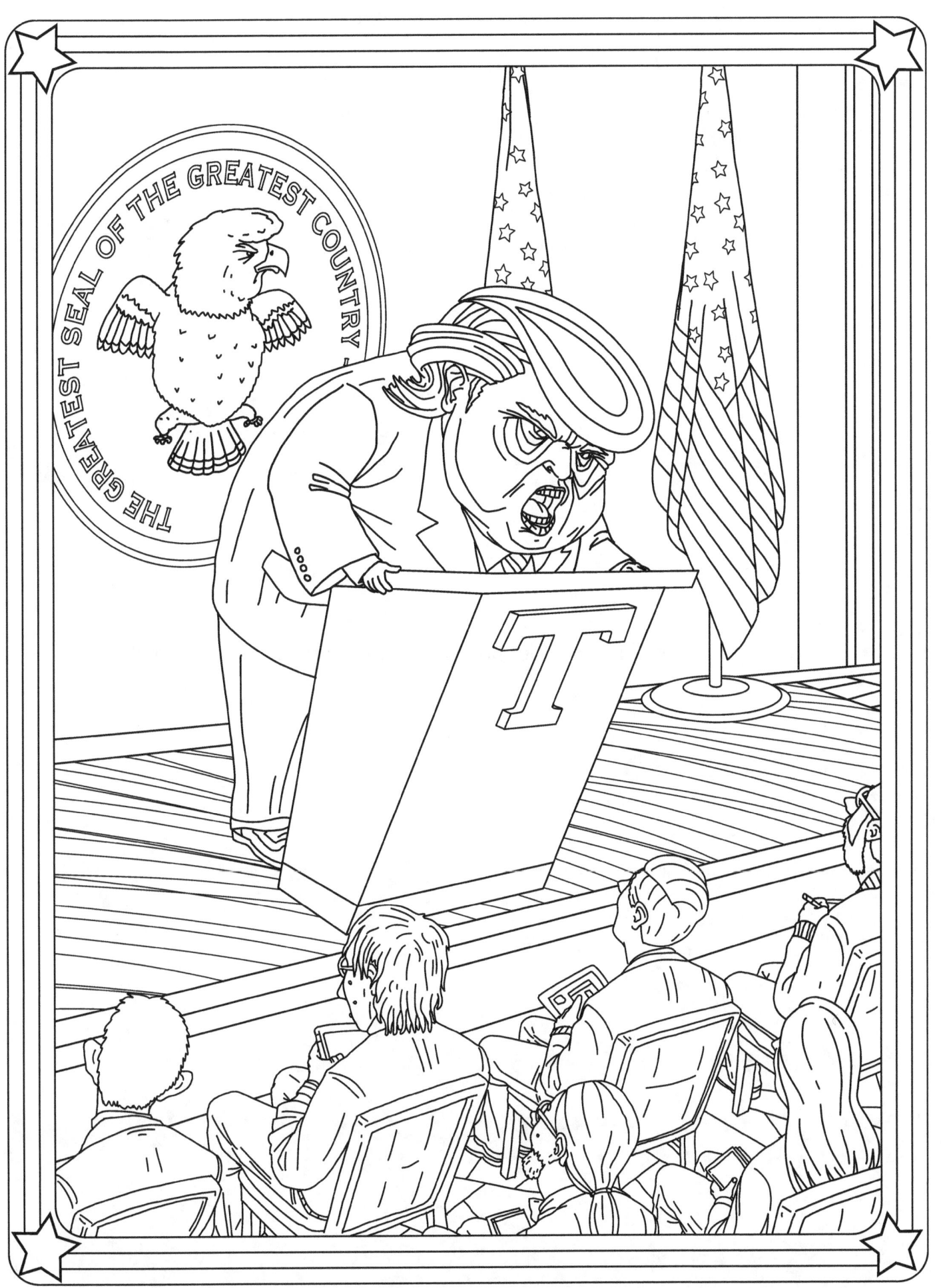

"Really? You voted for my idiot brother but I have to beg you to clap?"

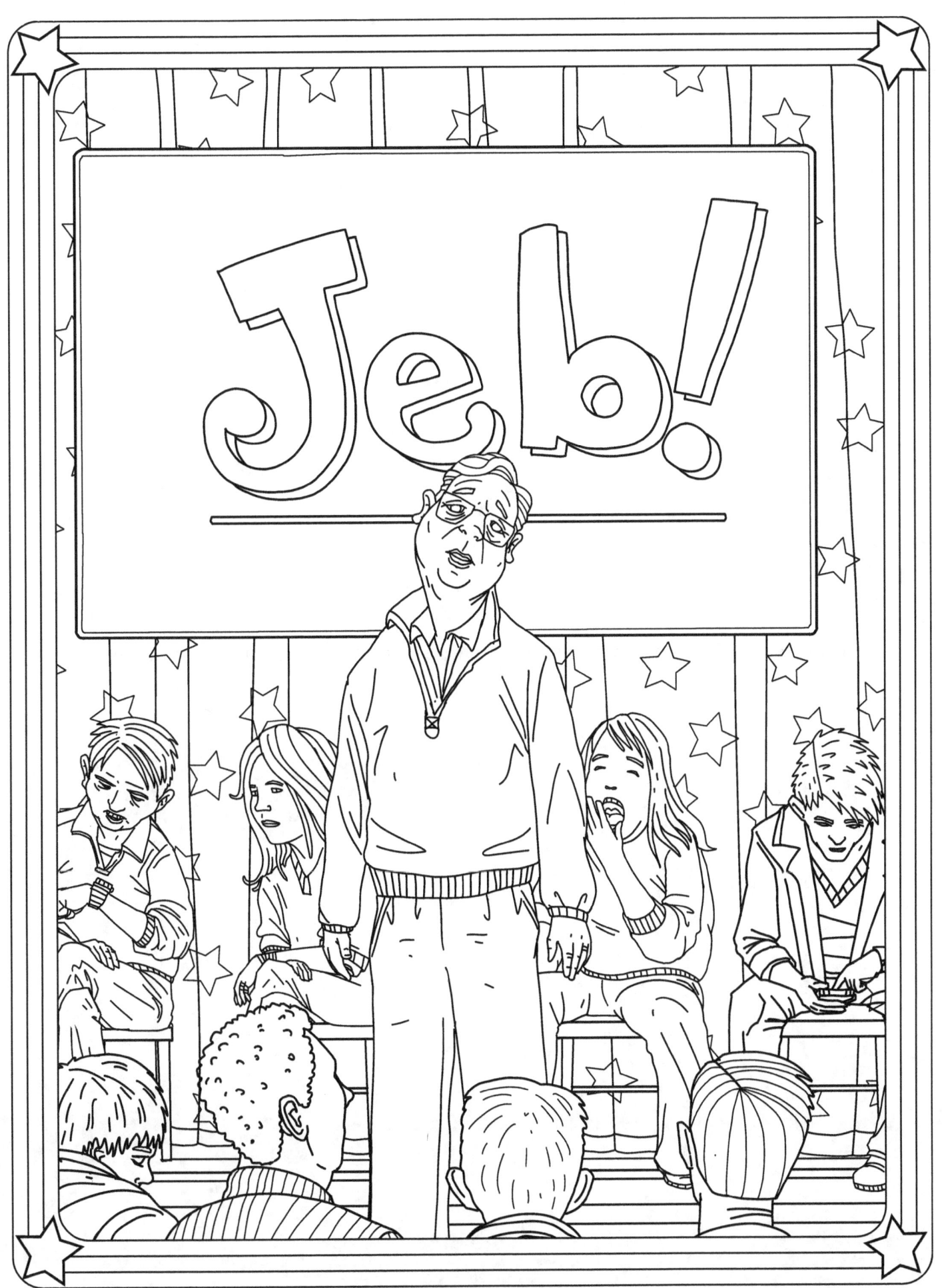

"Don't worry. I'm much better at brain surgery than I am at running for office."

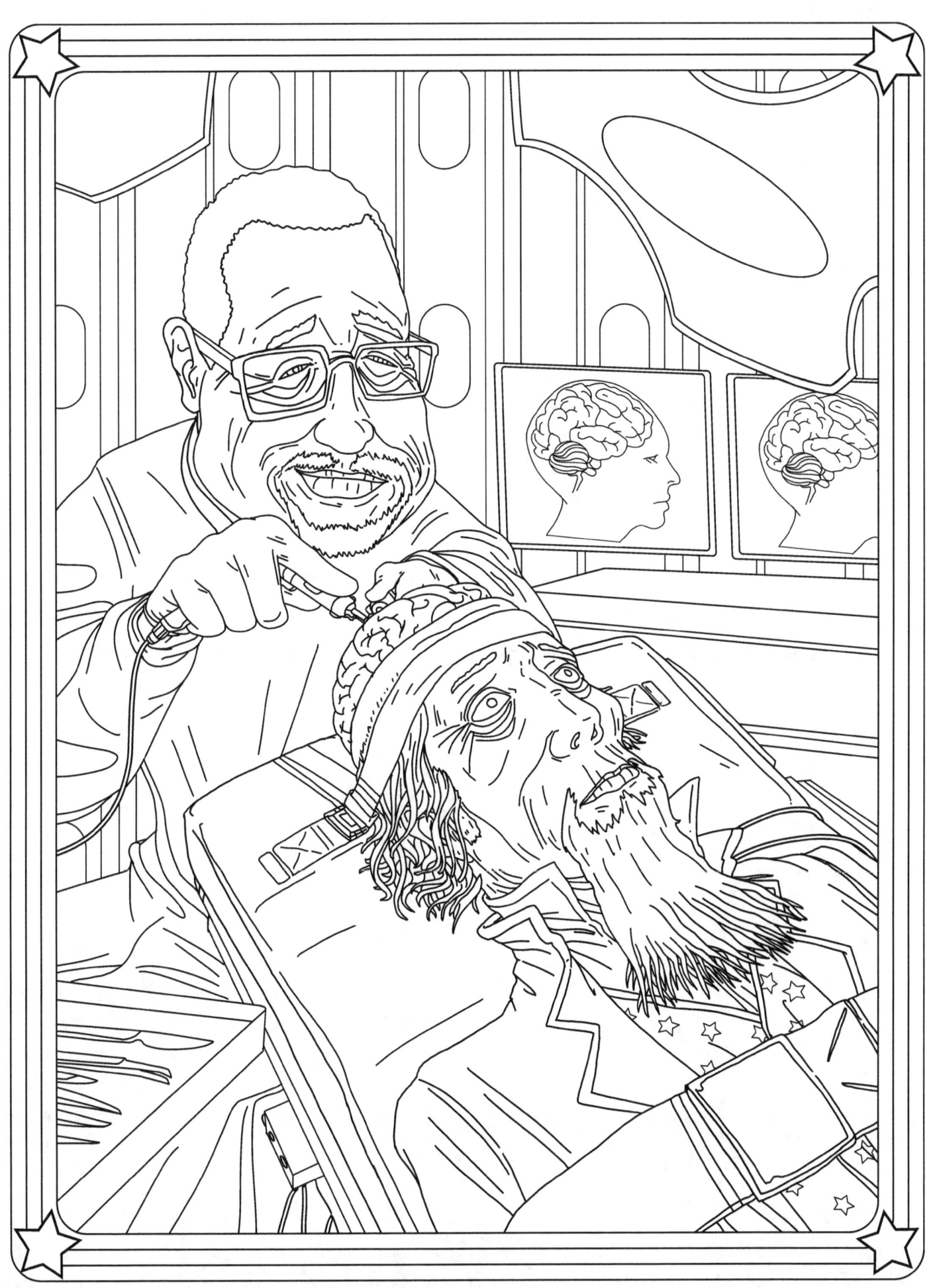

"Oh well. At least they'll mention my presidential bid in my obituary. I hope."

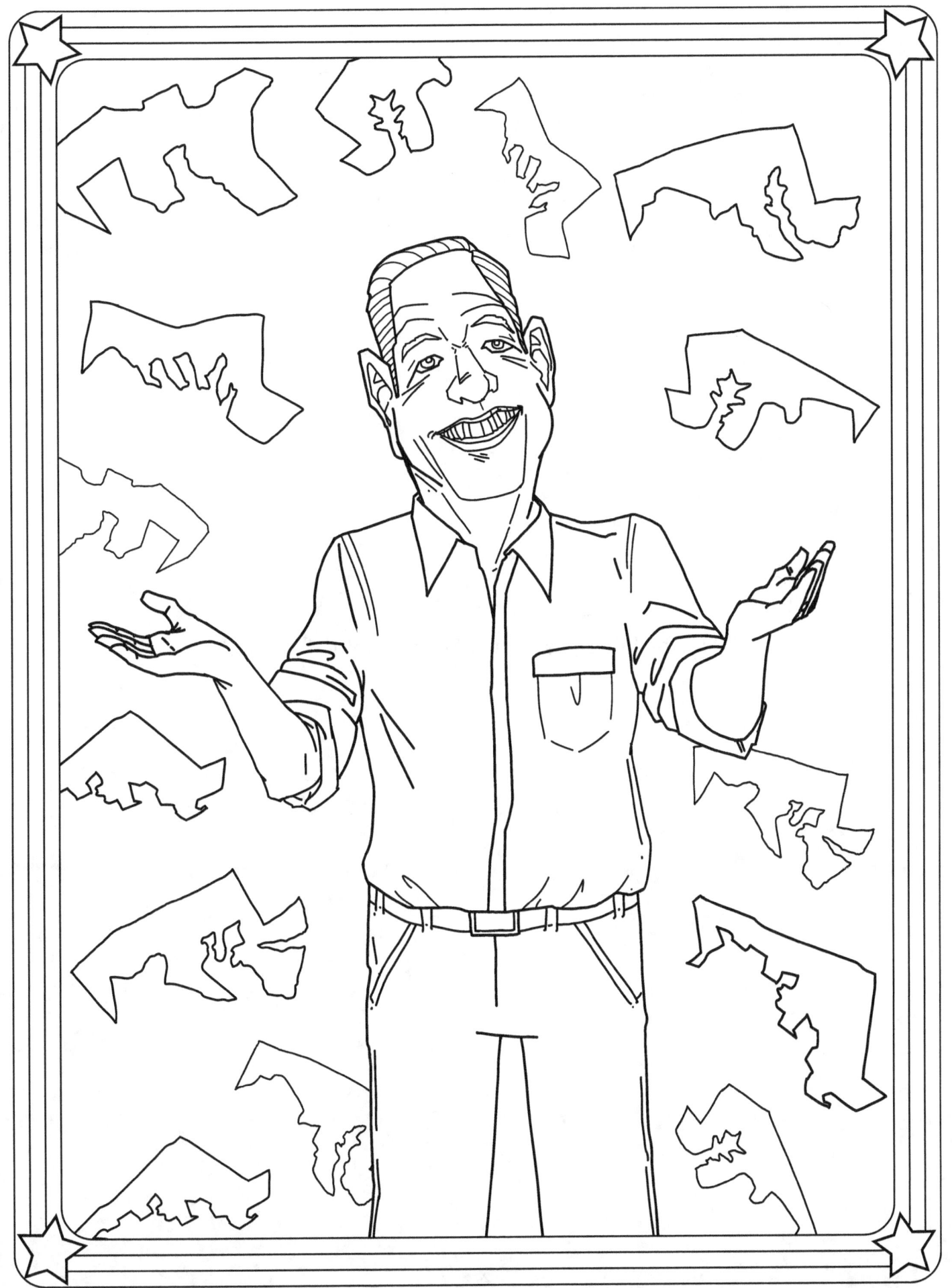

"If loving Liberty is wrong, I don't want to be right!"

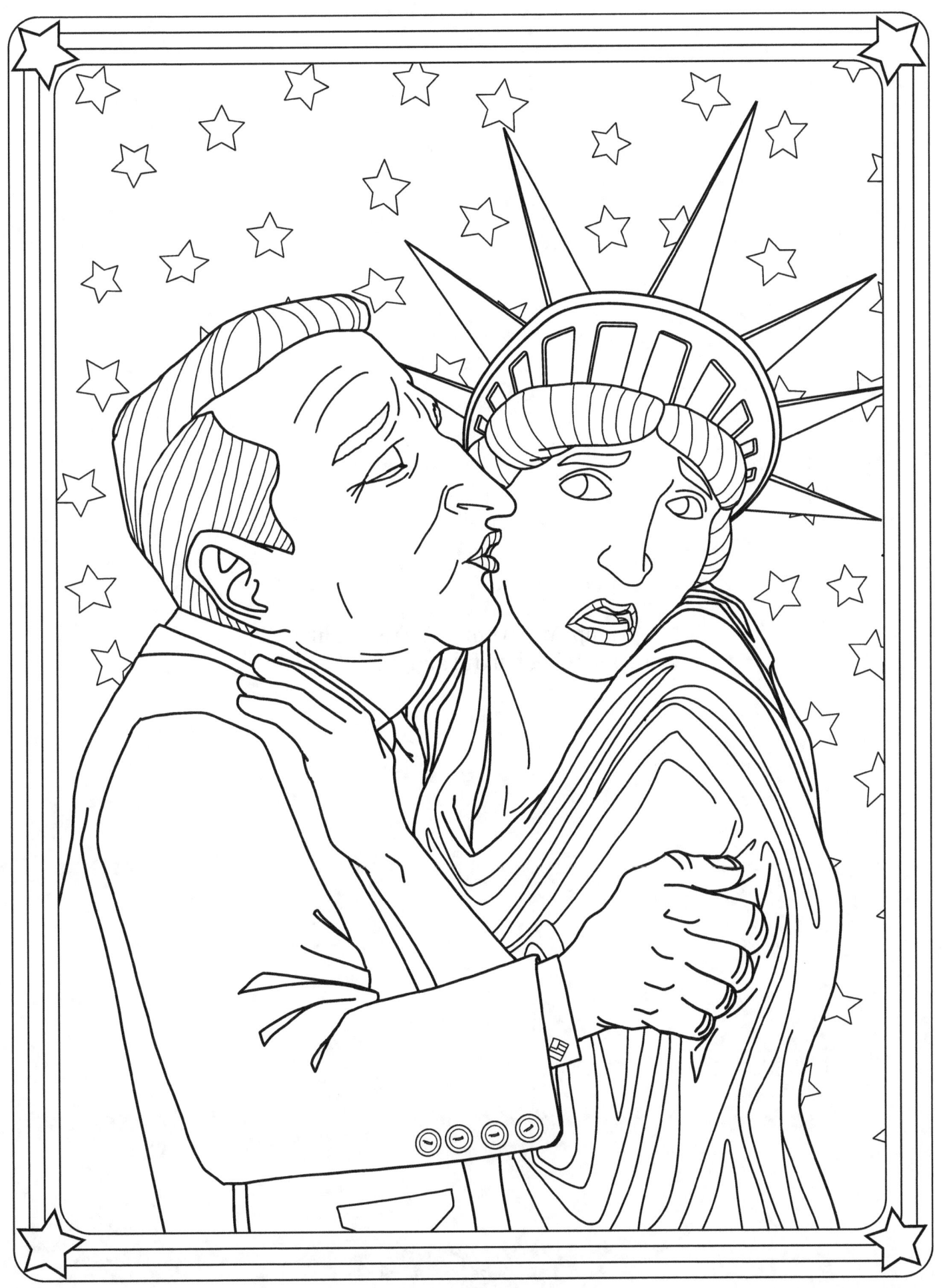

"Mr. Trump, Mr. Trump! You're just like us!
Say something hurtful and xenophobic!"

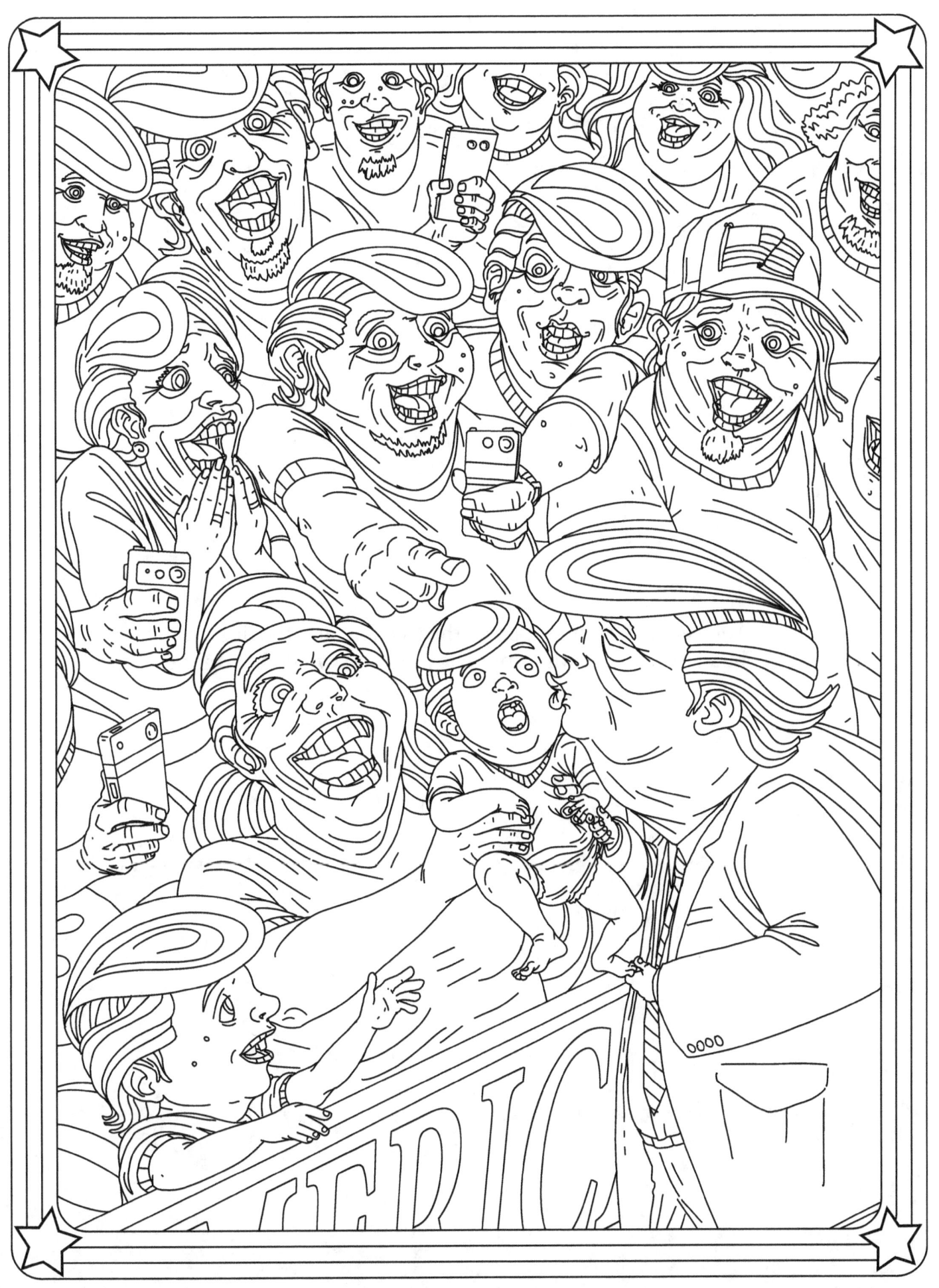

"You betcha! Trump supports the freedom and the liberty.
The Founders knew he who would be greatness would be America!"

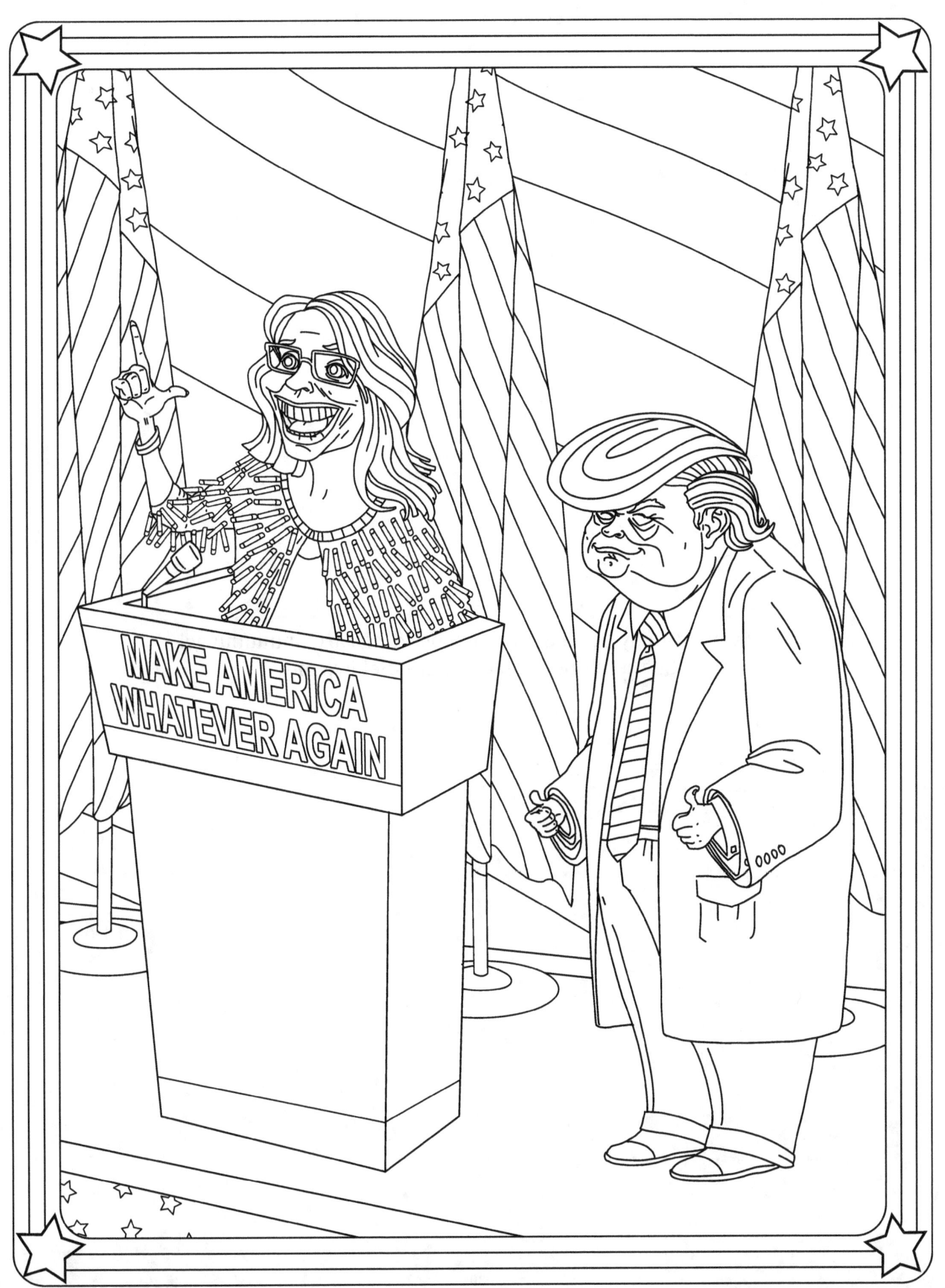

"My hands may be small, but my buildings are huuuuuuuge!
So there's no problem there. Believe me."

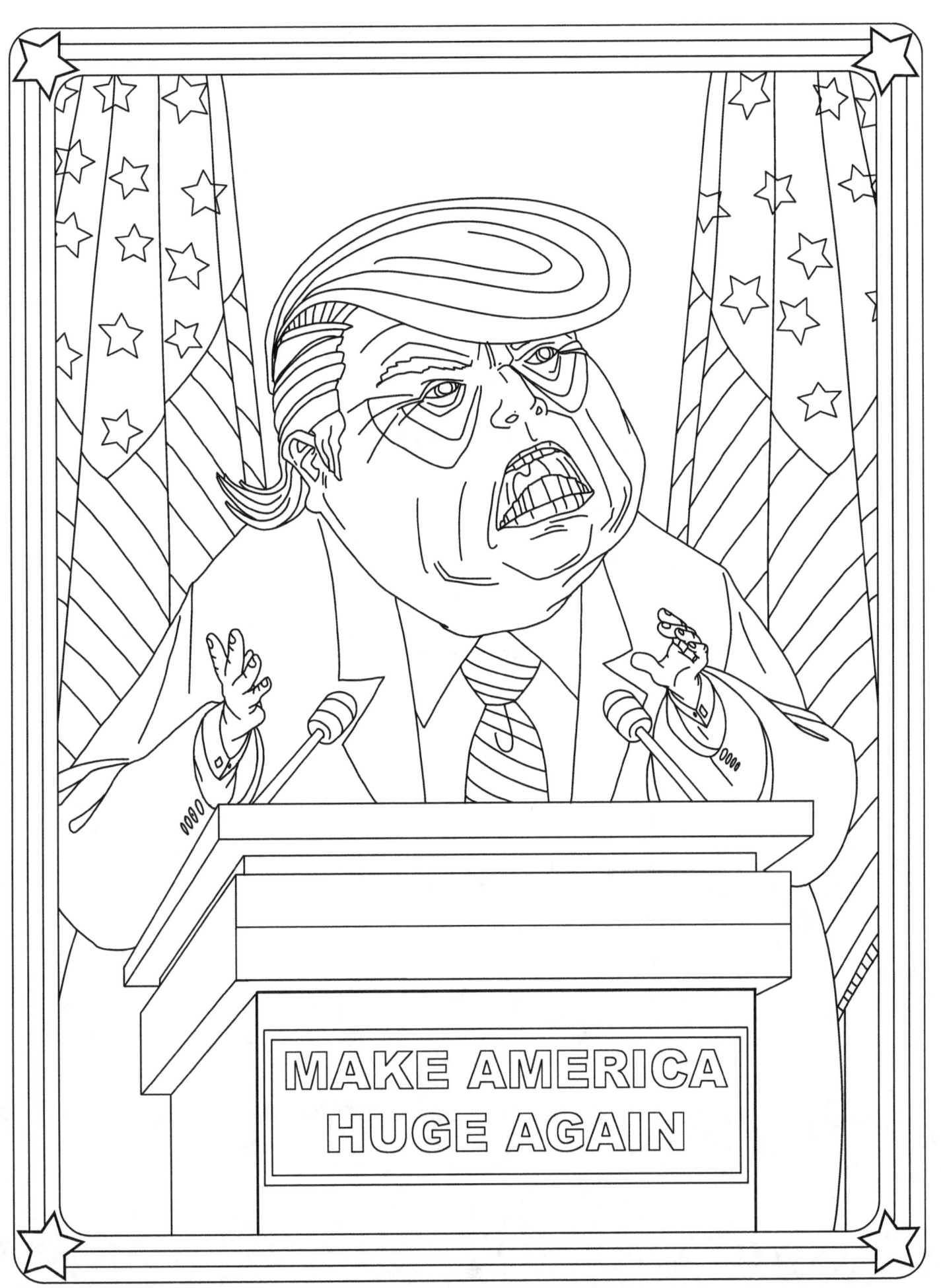

"You're fired!"

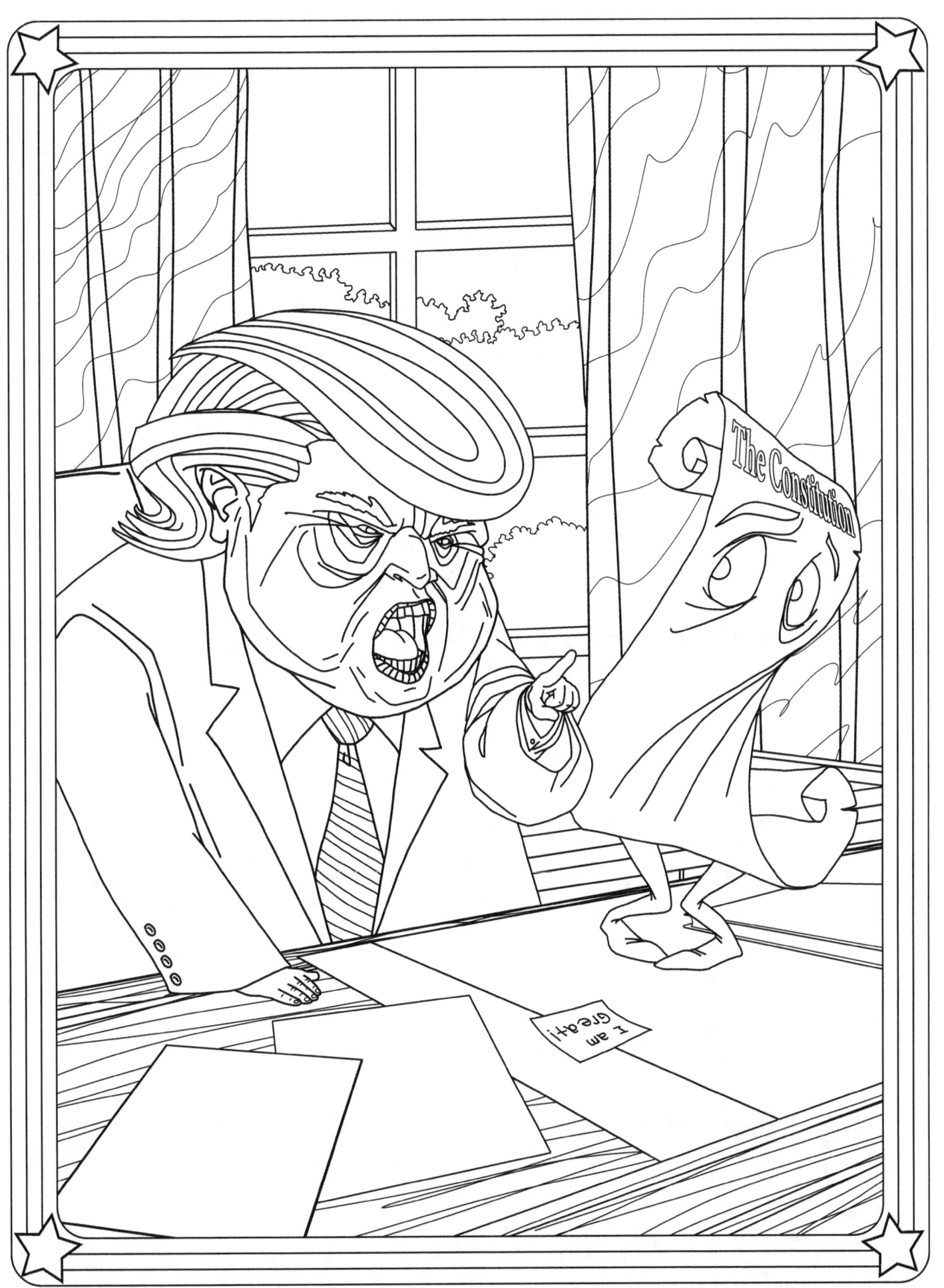

"Every American has the right to free health care, a free college education, and at least one unicorn."

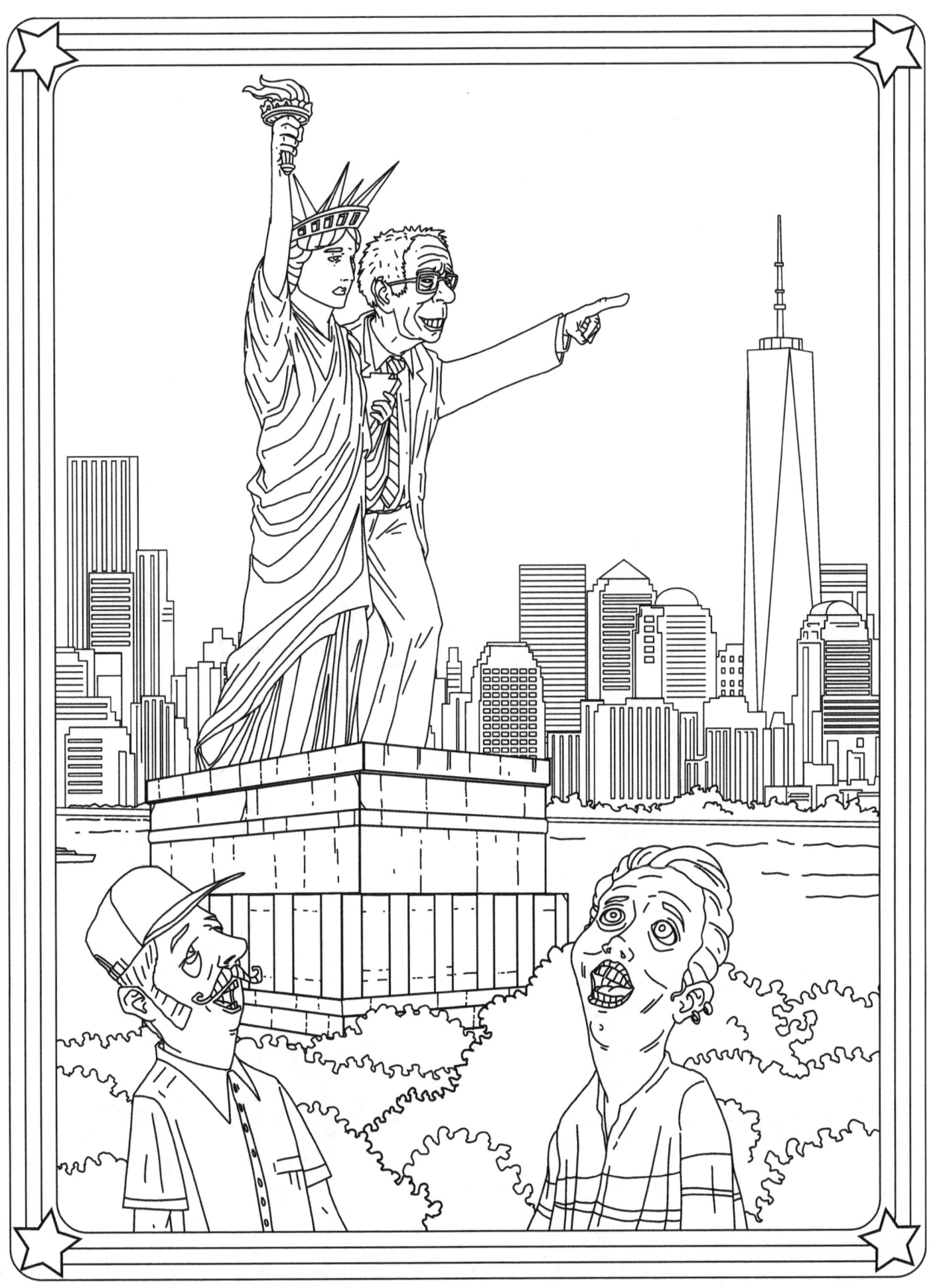

"When I hit send, these things just disappear, right?"

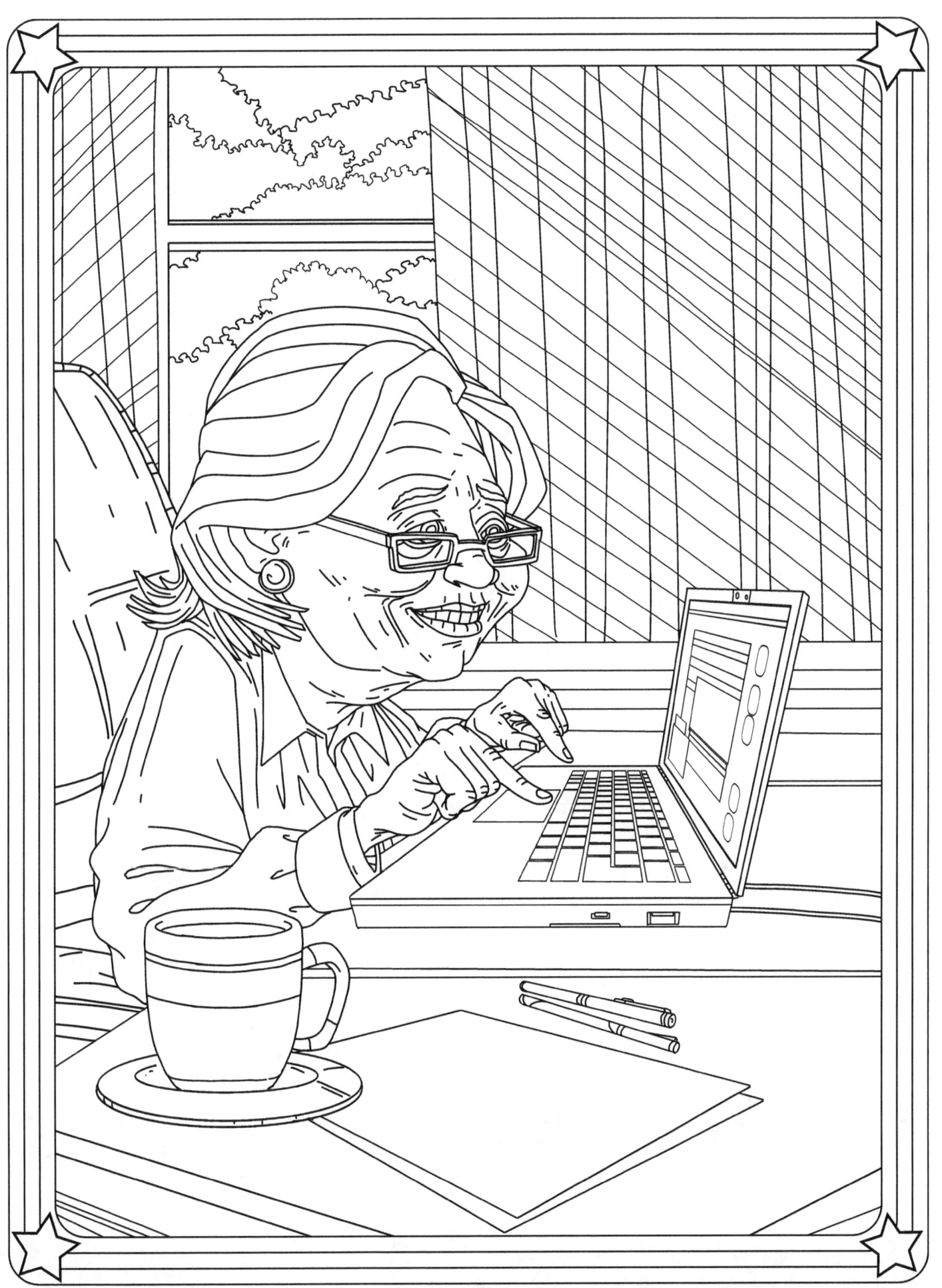

"Bring on the interns."

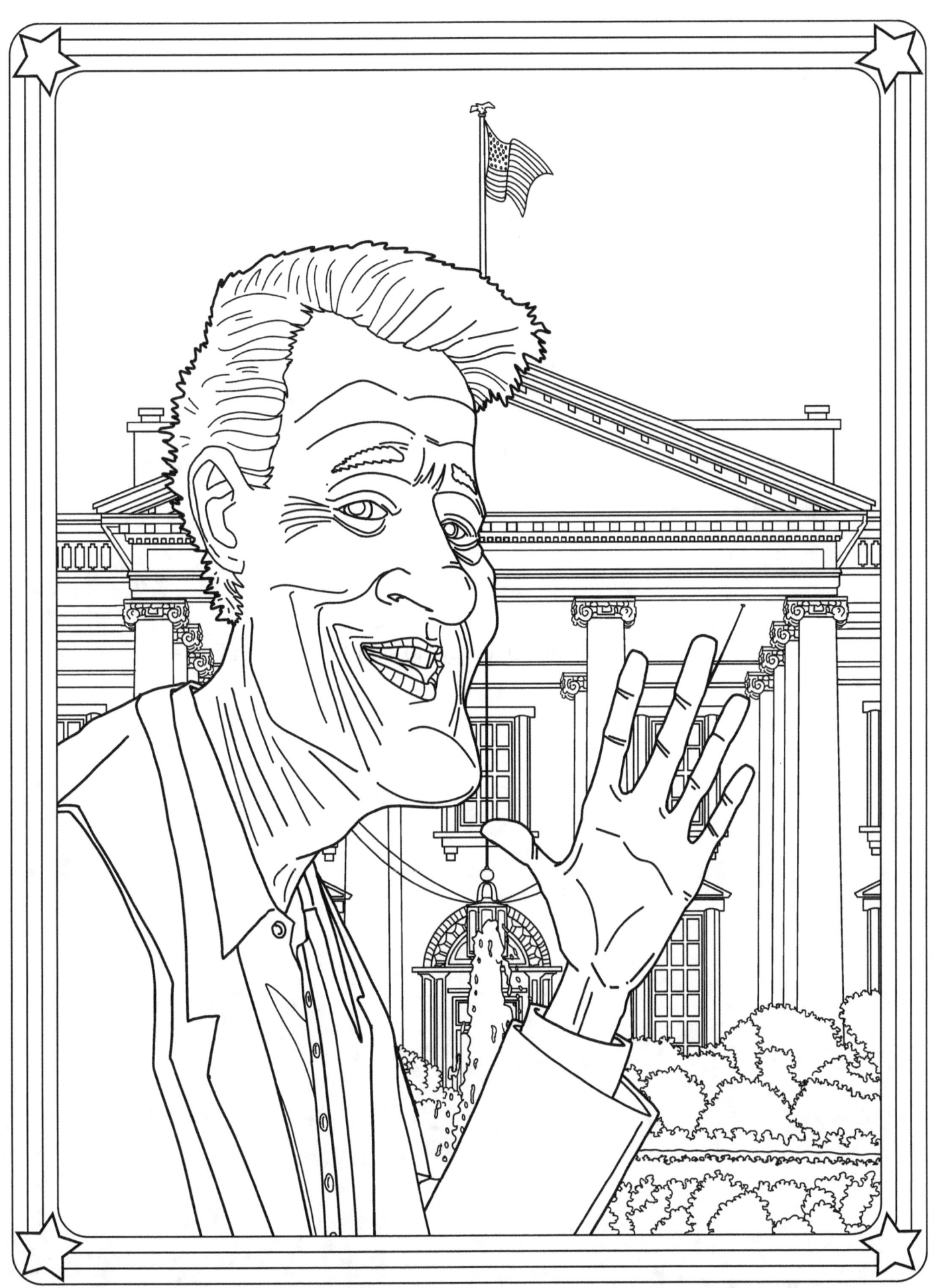

Add four years of "presidential gray" to your favorite candidates!

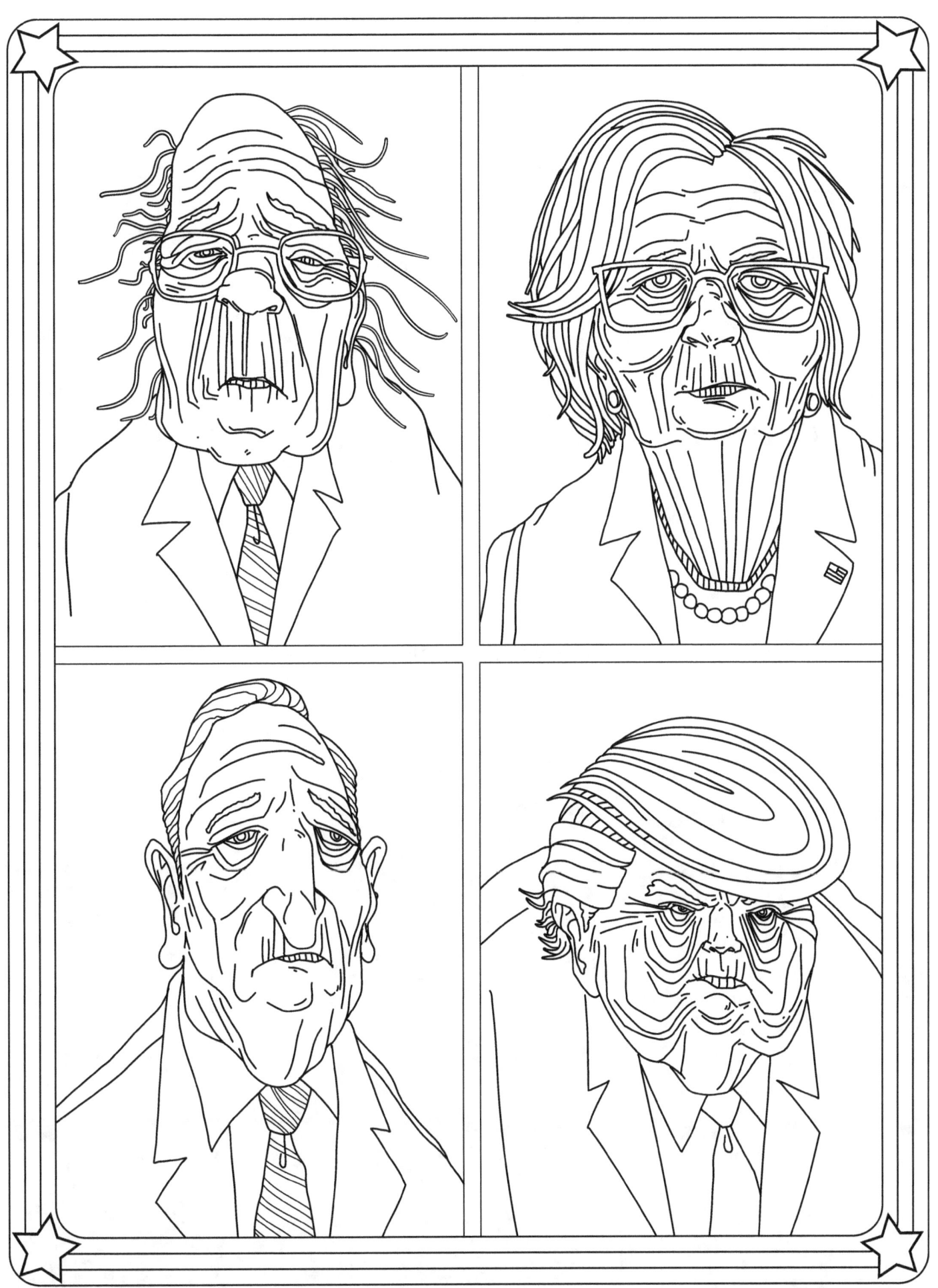

"We may have to build a wall."

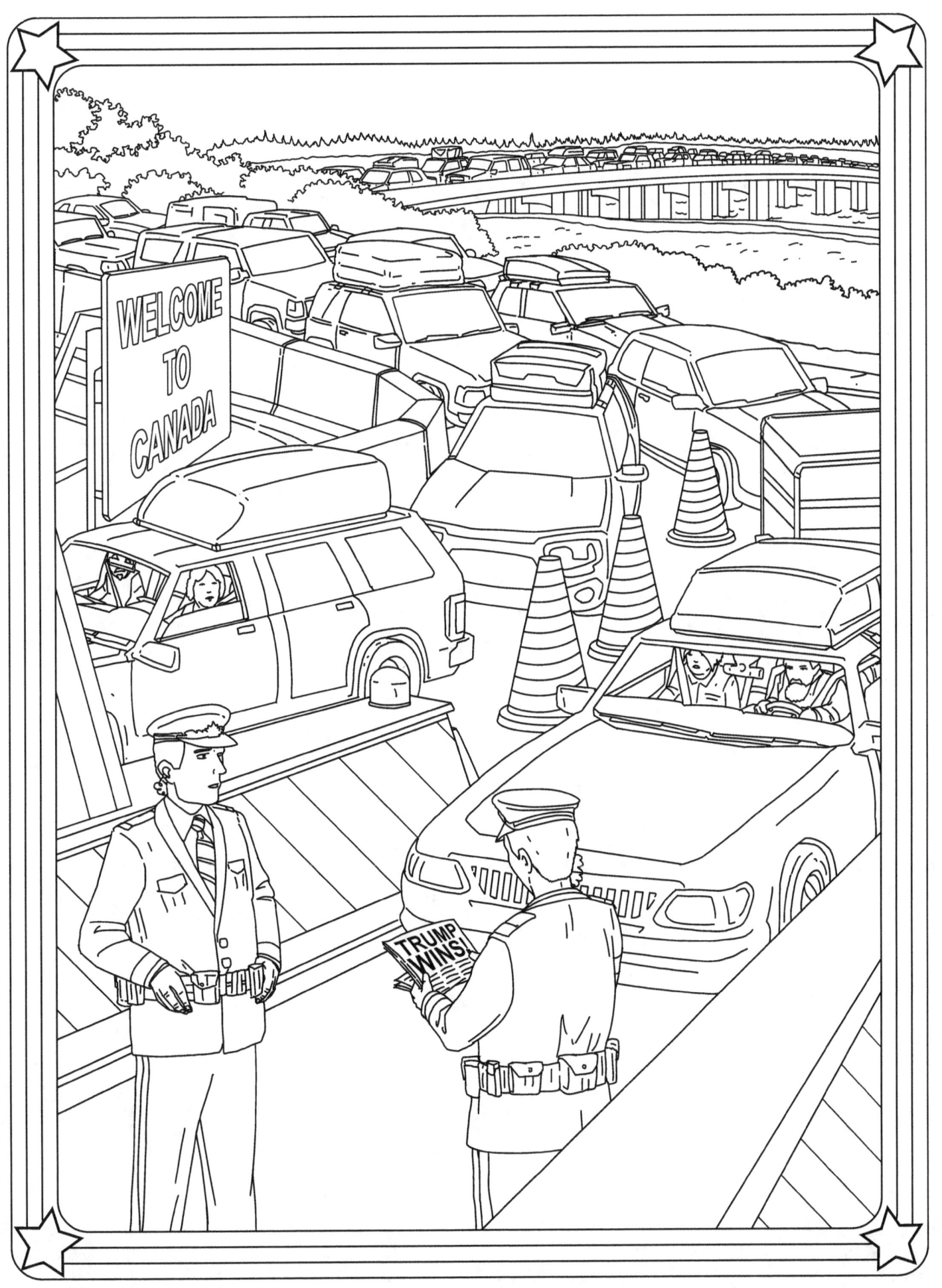

"You're a liar!"

"Can't I talk?!"

"Waaaaah!"

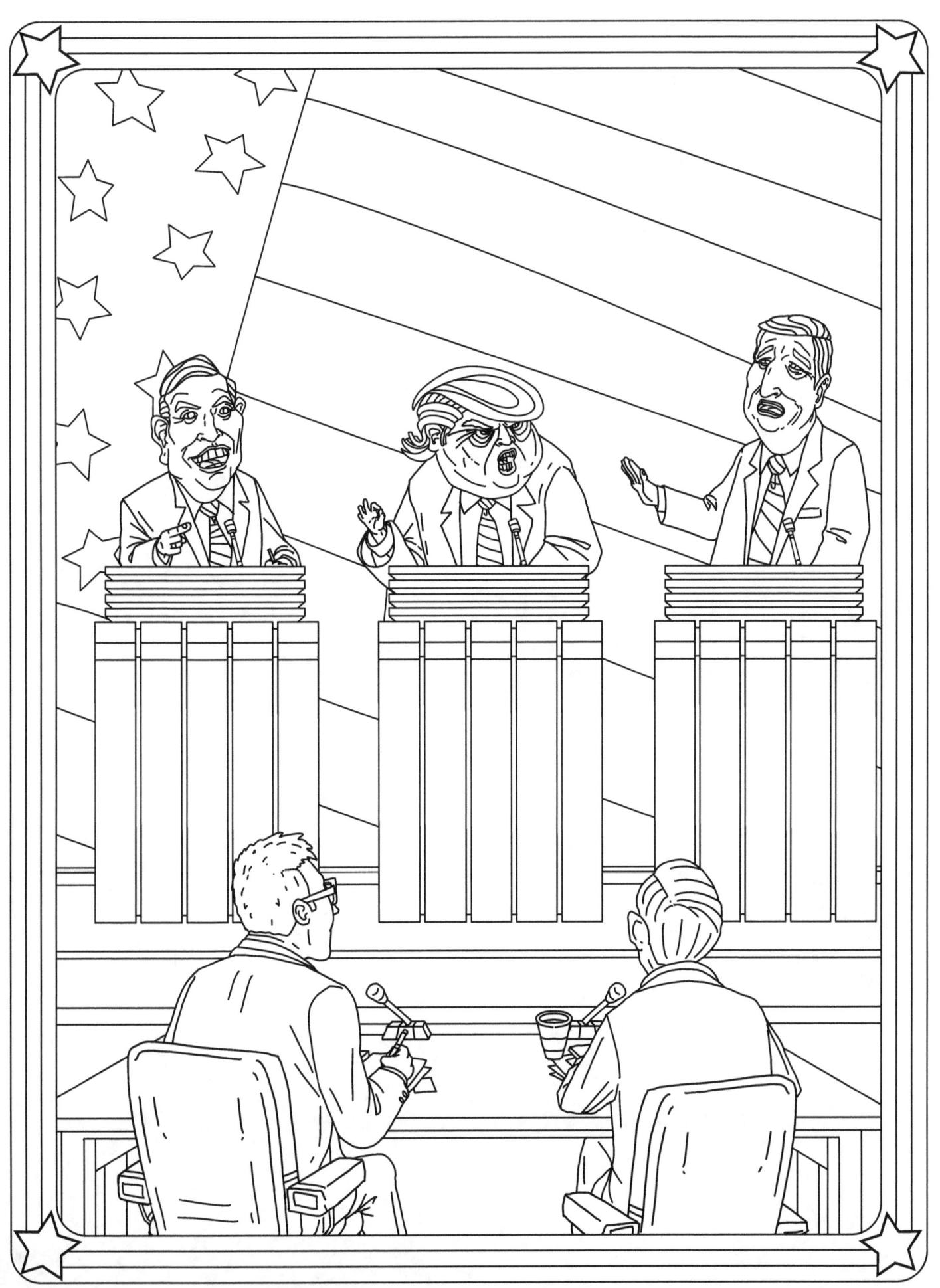

In Trump We Trust

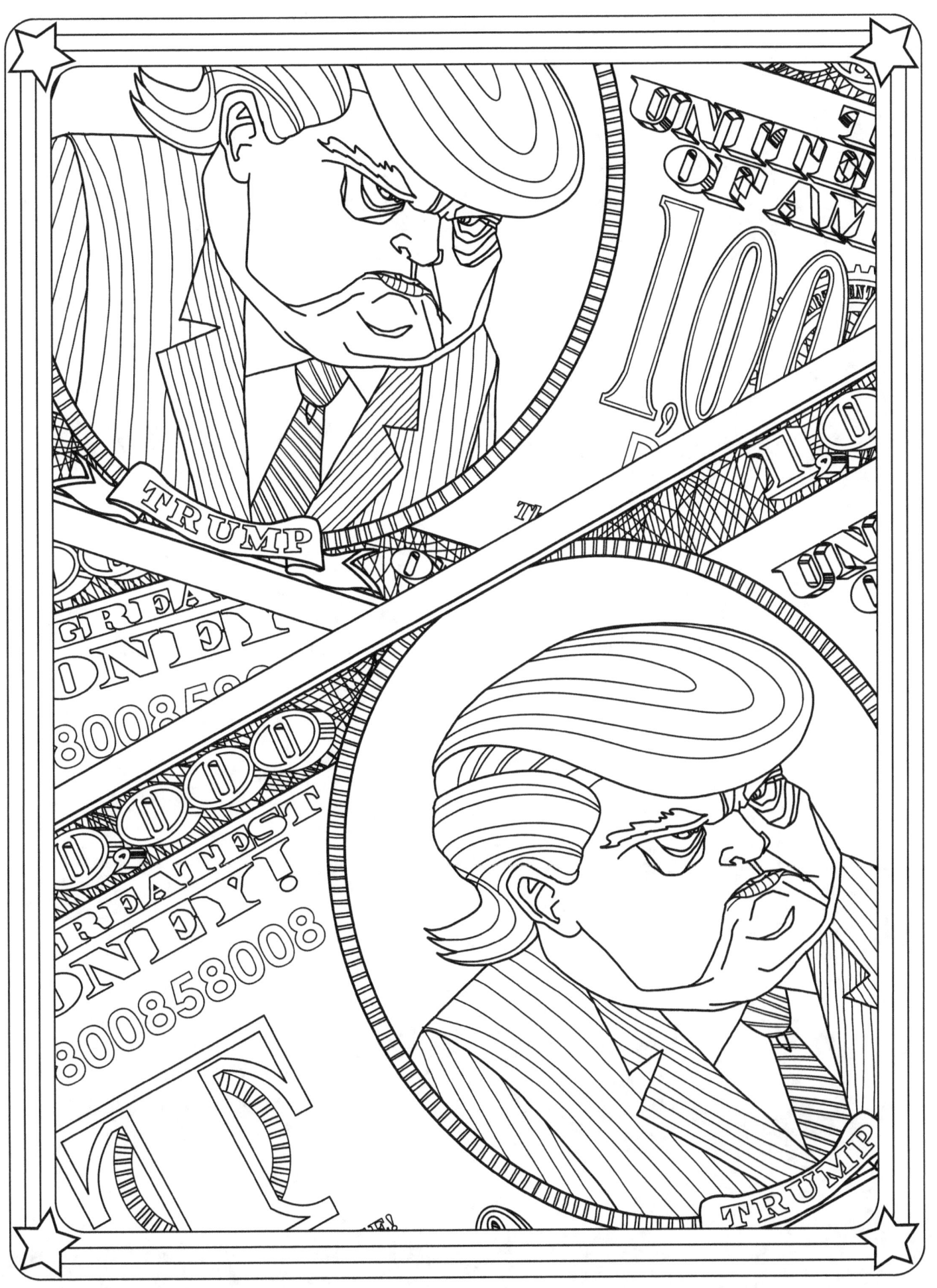

"Swipe Right if you believe in securing the border and religious liberty."

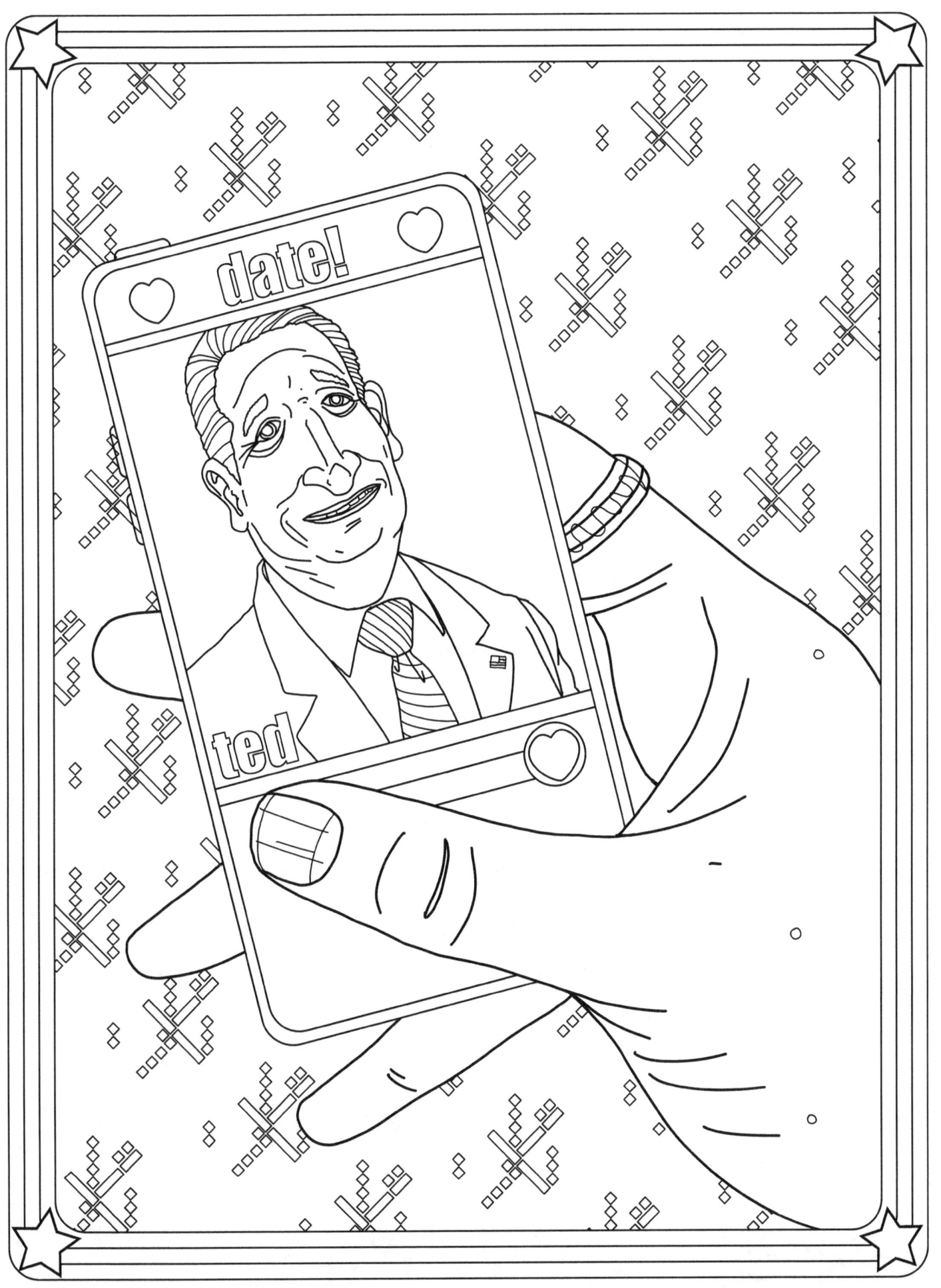

"Holy s*@t! What have we done?"

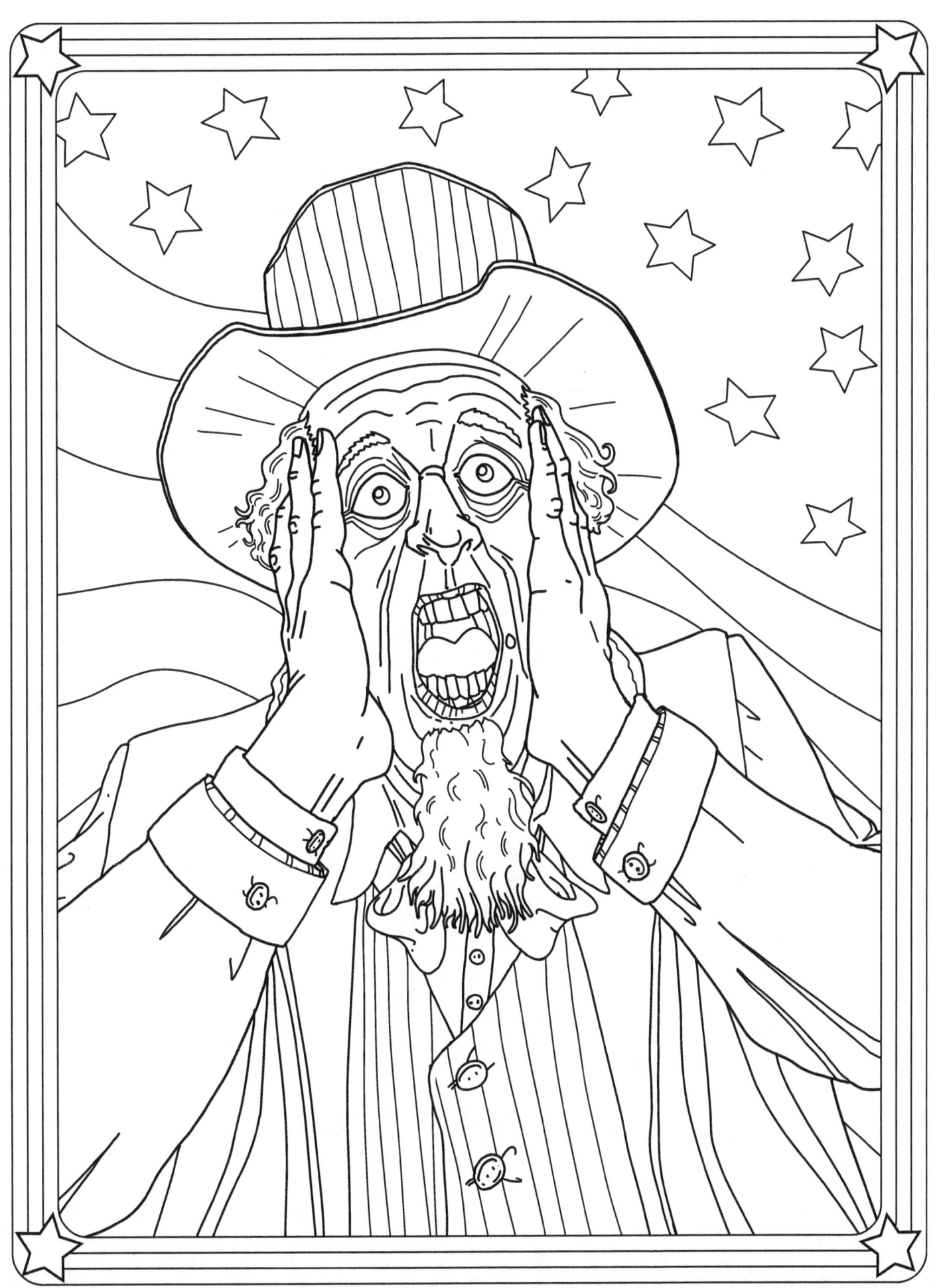

Dave Metrick is a project manager and freelance writer who is often frustrated with spineless politicians, the ridiculousness of modern media coverage, and an electorate who wants to have its cake and eat it too. When he's not busy complaining, he blogs about running as the Reluctant Runner (runningreluctant.com).

Todd Kale is an illustrator who misses the days when outlandish political rants were only found on late night AM radio conspiracy talk shows. His work is at toddkale.com.